IMAGES OF W

THE CRUSHING OF ARMY GROUP NORTH 1944-1945

RARE PHOTOGRAPHS FROM WARTIME ARCHIVES

Ian Baxter

Pen & Sword
MILITARY

First published in Great Britain in 2017 by
PEN & SWORD MILITARY
An imprint of
Pen & Sword Books Ltd
47 Church Street
Barnsley
South Yorkshire
S70 2AS

ISBN 978-1-47386-255-5

Typeset by Concept, Huddersfield, West Yorkshire HD4 5JL.
Printed and bound by CPI Group (UK) Ltd, Croydon, CR0 4YY

Pen & Sword Books Ltd incorporates the imprints of Pen & Sword Archaeology, Atlas, Aviation, Battleground, Discovery, Family History, History, Maritime, Military, Naval, Politics, Railways, Select, Social History, Transport, True Crime, and Claymore Press, Frontline Books, Leo Cooper, Praetorian Press, Remember When, Seaforth Publishing and Wharncliffe.

For a complete list of Pen & Sword titles please contact
PEN & SWORD BOOKS LIMITED
47 Church Street, Barnsley, South Yorkshire S70 2AS, England
E-mail: enquiries@pen-and-sword.co.uk
Website: www.pen-and-sword.co.uk

Contents

About the Author

Ian Baxter is a military historian who specialises in German twentieth century military history. He has written more than twenty books including *Afrika-Korps*; *Auschwitz Death Camp*; *Belsen and its Liberation*; *Blitzkrieg in the West*; *The Crushing of Poland*; *Final Days of the Reich*; *German Army on the Eastern Front – The Advance*; *German Army on the Eastern Front – The Retreat 1943–1945*; *German Guns of the Third Reich*; *Himmler's Nazi Concentration Camp Guards*; *Hitler's Defeat on the Eastern Front*; *Hitler's Headquarters 1939–1945*; *Hitler's Heavy Panzers 1943–45*; *Hitler's Mountain Troops 1939–1945: The Gebirgsjager*; *Hitler's Panzers*; *Nazi Concentration Camp Commandants 1933–1945*; *Panzer Divisions at War 1939–1945*; *Retreat to Berlin*; *The U-Boat War 1939–1945*; *Waffen-SS on the Eastern Front 1941–1945* and *Waffen-SS on the Western Front 1940–1945*. He has written over 100 journals including *Last days of Hitler, Wolf's Lair, Story of the V1 and V2 Rocket Programme, Secret Aircraft of World War Two, Rommel at Tobruk, Hitler's War with his Generals, Secret British Plans to Assassinate Hitler, SS at Arnhem, Hitlerjugend, Battle of Caen 1944, Gebirgsjäger at War, Panzer Crews, Hitlerjugend Guerrillas, Last Battles in the East, The Battle of Berlin*, and many more. He has also reviewed numerous military studies for publication, supplied thousands of photographs and important documents to various publishers and film production companies worldwide, and lectures to various schools, colleges and universities throughout the United Kingdom and Ireland.

Chapter One

A Brief History

At dawn on 22 June 1941, along an 1,800-mile-long invasion front, 3 million German soldiers on the frontier of the Soviet Union unleashed one of the most brutal conflicts of the twentieth century – Operation Barbarossa. Directing this invasion of Russia was Feldmarschall Ritter von Leeb, commander of *Heeresgruppe Nord* (Army Group North), Feldmarschall Fedor von Bock in the centre and Feldmarschall Gerd von Rundstedt in the south. Von Leeb's *Heeresgruppe Nord* was given the task of destroying the Red Army fighting in the Baltic region. Hitler stipulated on the eve of the invasion that the German objective was to thrust across East Prussia, smashing Soviet positions along the Baltic, liquidating the bases of the Baltic Fleet, destroying what was left of Russian naval power and capturing Kronstadt and Leningrad. Once the city had been razed to the ground, the German armies could sweep down from the north while the main force closed in from the west. With 500,000 men at Leeb's disposal, comprising almost thirty divisions, six of them armoured and motorized with 1,500 Panzers and 12,000 heavy weapons, plus an air fleet of nearly 1,000 planes, he was determined to strike along the Baltic coast and dispose of the Russian force once and for all.

Leeb's rapid two-pronged offensive along the Baltic opened up at first light on the morning of 22 June 1941. His force, consisting of 16th and 18th Armies, smashed through the Soviet defences. Russian soldiers stood helpless in its path, too shocked to take action. Over the coming weeks, German troops of Army Group North continued to chew through enemy positions, heading through Lithuania, Latvia and Estonia, straight towards their objective – Leningrad. Fortunately, the earth was baked under the blistering summer heat and Leeb's army was able to advance rapidly through the Baltic states.

By 10 July, Leeb's units broke south of Pskov and rolled toward Luga. At the rate they were advancing, they would need no more than nine or ten days to reach the outskirts of Leningrad. But following their surge of success, the Wehrmacht were losing momentum. Not only were their supply lines being overstretched, but enemy resistance began to stiffen on the road to Leningrad. In a desperate attempt to blunt the German advance and prevent them from reaching the imperial city, brigades of Russian marines, naval units, and more than 80,000 men from the Baltic Fleet were hastily sent into action against Leeb's forces. These Russian soldiers were now the sole barrier between Leningrad and the Germans. Although the advance was hampered by these Russian forces, by the end of August 1941, Leeb's Panzers were finally within sight of Leningrad. The terrified civilians left inside the city walls were now going to endure one of the most brutal sieges in twentieth century history.

As the summer of 1941 passed and the Germans drew closer to the city gates, Leningraders were given the grim order to defend their city to the death. Although Leeb's forces had arrived within shelling distance of Leningrad, the advance had not gone as planned. Already units had been badly disrupted and were mired on the Leningrad Front by stiffening resistance.

By 17 September, the Moscow Front could wait no longer for victory in the north. The shift of the main weight, the powerful 41.Panzer-Korps which Leeb required to sledgehammer his way to the outskirts of Leningrad, was taken out of line and ordered to the Moscow Front. Without the 41st Panzer Corps the whole dynamics of Army Group North had altered. There would now be no attack on Leningrad. Instead, Hitler ordered that the city would be encircled and the inhabitants defending inside would be starved to death. During October and November 1941, some ten German divisions were tied down around the city. For the next year German troops of Army Group North fought a series of bloody battles to hold their positions around Leningrad. Although they had managed to blunt Russian penetrations through their lines with the sacrifice of thousands of men killed and wounded, the battle had in fact absorbed all the available resources of the 18th Army and elements of the 11th Army, which had resulted in the planned assault on Leningrad being abandoned.

Now, a sense of futility and gloom gripped the German soldier in Army Group North. Thousands of soldiers had been killed and by mid-October 1942, they found themselves substantially in the same position they had been in spring. From the Volkhov River to the Gulf of Finland the front was reminiscent of the First World War – with a string of trenches and shell holes in which gains and losses could be measured only in yards. Because of defeats in southern Russia, German forces were now compelled to go on the defensive against growing resistance. Despite the prevailing conditions and the daily shelling, Leningrad gradually regained strength and became a strong fortress, capable of withstanding a further year and a half of siege and every enemy attempt to destroy it. Costly as this defence was, it managed to pin down huge parts of Army Group North that were desperately needed elsewhere to plug the crumbling front. When news of the Red Army's breakthrough came on 18 January 1943, it was greeted by soldiers of Army Group North with trepidation. From their relatively inactive front they watched anxiously as the Russians began increasing their attacks. Commanders in the field were well aware that if the hold on Leningrad were broken, Army Group North would eventually lose control of the Baltic Sea. Finland would be isolated; supplies of iron ore from Sweden would be in danger, and the U-boat training programme would be seriously curtailed. It was now imperative that the troops held the front and waged a static battle of attrition until other parts of the Russian front could be stabilized.

By the summer of 1943, the front continued to hold. Frontline German strength in July was 710,000 men. Army Group North was also building up a huge number of reserves echeloned in depth behind the northern fronts in the Baltic states of Estonia and Latvia. Both the Germans and Soviets in northern Russia were almost equal in strength, but the Red Army was also known to have substantial reserves and were building up significant forces to weaken Army Group North's defensive battles around Leningrad and Nevel. The Germans tried their best to hold the lines by shifting Luftwaffe field divisions and SS units newly recruited in the Baltic states.

(This and the following 2 pages) Five photographs showing Wehrmacht troops in Army Group North during operations on the Eastern Front with inflatable assault boats. The German assault boat was used by combat soldiers for mainly inland water operations. It was light enough to be carried by several troops to the rivers, lakes and other inland water areas where they could be either paddled or fitted with outboard motors to move from one part of the water to another.

(*Opposite above*) A heavy MG 34 machine gun position on a sustained fire mount. In open terrain the MG 34 machine gun squad would use their sustained fire mount to protect the flanks of advancing rifle companies.

(*Above*) Infantry with their standard armament – the Karabiner 98K bolt action rifle – prepare to move forward into action. When in line normally, two battalions would be forward and one in reserve; however, when the front line was being overstretched it was not uncommon to have all three on the front.

(*Opposite below*) Wehrmacht troops take cover in a position heavily concealed by undergrowth. Foliage has been attached to their M35 steel helmets for additional concealment.

The Flammenwerfer 35, or FmW 35 (flame thrower) in operation in Army Group North. This weapon was a one-man flamethrower used by the Germans primarily to clear out trenches, buildings, bunkers and other positions where the enemy is difficult to remove. The flame thrower could project fuel up to 25 metres. It weighed 35.8 kilograms and held 11.8 litres of oil and petrol mixed with tar. The tar was to make it heavier and give it better range. It was ignited by a hydrogen torch providing about ten seconds of continuous use.

Infantrymen stand beside a shelter during operations in Army Group North. The shelters which the Germans built were called *Halbgruppenunterstande* (half-group living bunkers). These were to become essential for the Landser to survive the ceaseless artillery bombardments and freezing weather conditions of the Eastern Front.

Two photographs showing the appalling road conditions caused by rain and the constant flow of heavy traffic. In the first photograph Wehrmacht troops cling to the side of a halftrack as they negotiate the vehicle along a typical muddy road in the summer of 1941 in Army Group North. A quick downpour of rain could quickly turn a dry road into a quagmire and grind columns of wheeled vehicles to a halt.

A BMW motorcyclist with sidecar combination halts on a road. Note the WH painted either in yellow or white on the front of the sidecar, this denotes the vehicle is attached to the Wehrmacht. In the background, buildings have been set ablaze.

This whitewashed 15cm howitzer has been positioned out in a field and is already embroiled in a firing mission against an enemy target. The gun could be traversed 64 degrees (32 degrees each side of the centre line), and could fire a projectile miles into enemy lines with considerable destructive power.

Out in the field and being used against a ground target is the lethal quadruple 2cm flak gun. During the war these formidable weapons were found in a number of Wehrmacht mechanized flak battalions, and divisions also had additional anti-aircraft platoons and companies in their Panzergrenadier, Panzer and artillery regiments.

The crew of a whitewashed 10.5cm heavy field howitzer is positioned in the snow with the crew preparing their gun for a fire mission. Placed at distance, ammunition can be seen stacked in special crates. On the Eastern Front artillery gunners soon learned from combat experience that artillery support was of decisive importance in both defensive and offensive roles.

During winter operations two soldiers can be seen wearing their snow camouflage garments while sitting on their shelter. Note the array of weaponry leaning against an earth mound near to their position. One of the weapons is a captured Soviet PPSh-41 sub-machine gun.

A 5cm Granatwerfer 36 mortar crew during winter combat. This weapon fired a very light shell that often fell short of its target. Production of this weapon was terminated in 1941, but it was still widely used on the Eastern Front during this period. By 1942, it was gradually phased out of frontline service, but it remained with second-line and garrison units, especially for training purposes.

Soviet troops wearing snow camouflage two-piece suits attacking a German position during winter operations in Army Group North during the first year of fighting on the Eastern Front.

In the depths of the Russian winter, a Soviet T-34 tank can be seen partially concealed in the snow after being knocked out of action.

(*Above*) In a dugout position, a German MG 34 machine gunner scours the terrain through a pair of 6 × 30 Zeiss binoculars trying to locate the position of the enemy. This light MG is being used from its bipod mount. With the bipod extended and the belt loaded, the machine gunner could move the weapon quickly from one position to another, and quickly throw it to the ground and put it into operation with deadly effect.

(*Opposite page*) A group of Wehrmacht soldiers showing their personal kit converse with their NCO. The troops are all wearing a two-piece winter reversible camouflage smock and black leather boots. For the second winter of 1942 a German Army reversible winter uniform was manufactured and supplied to the front lines. When the troops were issued with these garments in October and November 1942, they found the clothing warm and comfortable. The uniform also provided the wearer with greater freedom of movement, especially when encumbered with personal equipment. The uniform not only helped combat the cold, but also helped prevent overheating during physical exertion.

Chapter Two

Defensive Action

By the end of 1943 there was nothing but a string of defeats for the German Army as it fought like grim death to try to hold back the overwhelming might of the Russians. It was in the Baltic states where Army Group North played a decisive role in trying to stem the rout and prevent the fragile lines from finally being smashed. As the last remnants of Army Group North were driven back across a scarred and devastated wasteland to the borders of Estonia, Latvia and Lithuania, German troops were ordered to 'stand and fight' and wage an unprecedented battle of attrition.

The Army's tactical position had become very fragile and was made worse on 14 January 1944 when the Red Army launched its winter offensive against the Leningrad and Volkhov Fronts. The German 18th Army were outnumbered by at least 3:1 in divisions, 3:1 in artillery, and 6:1 in tanks, self-propelled artillery, and aircraft. Fighting was fierce and German troops were severely battered by overwhelming Soviet forces. General Georg von Küchler, the new commander of Army Group North, appealed to Hitler for a complete withdrawal, but Hitler responded angrily, prohibited all voluntary withdrawals and reserved all decisions to withdraw to himself. However, one week later, after the 18th Army had incurred more than 50,000 casualties, Hitler reluctantly approved a retreat to the Luga River but directed that the front be held, contact with 16th Army regained, and all gaps in the front closed.

Perturbed by Küchler's strategy, Hitler blamed the general for forcing his decision to withdraw. He decided to relieve Küchler of his command and replace him with his troubleshooter Generalfeldmarschall Walter Model. It was Model who ordered his 'Shield and Sword' policy, which stated that retreats were intolerable unless they paved the way for a counterstroke later. Now temporary commander of Army Group North, Model was given the awesome task of trying to minimize the extent of the disaster that was looming along the Baltic. It was here in the north that Model had the greatest opportunity to display his talents as an improviser. He immediately sent out an order to all commanders in the field that they were not to step backward. They were also to uphold the Führer's demands that troops were to build defence lines where they stood and fight to the bitter end.

Model was quite aware of the grave situation, and was even more conscious that the battle would soon spill over into Estonia. He envisaged that some of the bitterest battles on the Eastern Front would be fought along the borders and in the heartlands of this country.

On 2 February 1944, as the Red Army were bearing down along the frontier of Estonia, Model inspected the front and watched as his divisions were pulled back to the west bank of the Narva River in order to strengthen the city of Narva. Model was well aware of the geographical significance of Narva and its river line, which acted as a natural obstacle. The Germans had established quite a large and strongly defended bridgehead covering an area of territory on the eastern approaches to Narva. The Russians were determined to secure a bridgehead, and Model knew that his force would have to defend the river and the city to the bitter end to prevent the Soviets breaking into Estonia. For this reason, the Narva Front would have to be strengthened with the all possible speed if catastrophe was to be averted in this area. Here, soldiers from the SS Division 'Nordland' and Brigade 'Nederland' dug in and waited for the enemy assault. All available reserves were to be rushed to the front line and this included the release of an Estonian brigade. The brigade had been drafted by the Waffen-SS, which had been since January 1944 conducting an extensive recruitment programme in Estonia, Latvia and Lithuania. Many of the draftees were dispirited, their only motivation to fight alongside the Germans being that they feared reprisals against their own people.

On the Narva, the front was held by a mixture of well-armed and determined soldiers eager not to give one inch to their hated foe. For a number of days, a stalemate of sorts reigned along the river with both sides shelling each other's positions. In spite of dogged resistance by both German and foreign conscripts on 6 March the Russians began directing their firepower against Narva along the main road to Tallinn.

In the smoldering city of Narva the Germans continued resisting. Soviet air attacks mercilessly pounded the city while artillery from the 2nd Shock Army launched a fierce unremitting attack at three weakened German regiments defending the city, firing some 100,000 shells and grenades. The 'Nederland' Brigade took the brunt of the main attack, but the troops were able temporarily to blunt the advance along the river. Two days later a heavy assault was launched northwest from Narva, bitterly defended by the 4th SS Brigade's 49th Regiment of the SS-Freiwilligen Panzergrenadier Regiment 'de Ruyter'. For hours both sides duelled. The fighting was so fierce that the attack disintegrated into hand-to-hand battles between advancing Soviet infantry and vastly outnumbered Dutch troops of the 49th SS Regiment. After several hours of combat, the Soviets withdrew with high losses and decided to shift their attack elsewhere.

Over the next two weeks the 4th SS Brigade tried desperately not to fall back, despite being subjected to constant artillery and air attacks. In other parts of the front the 24th SS Regiment 'Danmark' of the 11th SS Division also received a mauling along with the 4th SS Brigade's 48th Regiment positioned to the south of the 24th SS Regiment. Fighting was intense and losses were massive resulting in the virtual annihilation of the 49th Regiment's 5th Company.

As parts of the German front began to crumble, the Russian Second Baltic Front stepped up its pressure against the divisions of the 16th Army, trying to punch a hole through its lines. Luckily for the Germans the weather had taken a turn for the worse. After a warm winter the spring thaw had set in early. A foot of water covered the ice on the surrounding lakes and Soviet tanks were sometimes sinking up to their turrets. In a number of places the roads were turned into quagmires making the advance painfully slow.

The Soviet setback enabled Model quickly to improvise, but as he set about increasing the defences on the Narva Front, Hitler posted his 'troubleshooter' to Army Group South. General George Lindemann was appointed acting commanding general of Army Group North. Lindemann was no defence expert, but he soon rallied his commanders in the field to ensure that the front held at all costs.

In the last week of March, Lindemann's dogged determination and fearlessness saw the Wehrmacht gain the initiative. After seven long weeks of fighting, the Soviet 2nd Shock Army were exhausted, were low on supplies, and had suffered too many casualties to mount any more large-scale operations. Consequently the Russian drive halted and the front line stagnated until May.

A column of vehicles comprising of wheeled support vehicles, motorcycle combinations and other forms of transportation used for the advance into the Russian heartlands.

(*Opposite above*) Moving along one of the many trenches that were dug along the front lines, Wehrmacht troops are seen wearing their two-piece winter reversible camouflage smocks and black toques. The toque was worn to retain heat lost through the wearer's head and keep his face and neck warm from the arctic elements.

(*Opposite below*) What appear to be Luftwaffe flak gunners out in the snow belonging to an unidentified 8.8cm flak battery in Army Group North. These gunners are wearing the familiar winter reversible. The winter reversible was normally mouse-grey on one side and winter white on the other. Soldiers often wore the garment depending on the terrain, and in this photograph they wear them grey side out, not concealing themselves very well against the white terrain. By the early winter of 1944, the winter reversible had become the most popular item of winter clothing worn by the troops on the Eastern Front. Soldier survivability had actually increased, in spite of the major military setbacks. In the winter of 1941 more than half the casualties were caused by the cold, often from frostbite. By the end of 1942, this figure had reduced considerably. Two years later, in the early winter of 1944, cold was responsible for less than a quarter of the casualties.

(*Above*) A 10.5cm artillery crew is in action against a Soviet position. The 10.5cm light field howitzer was used extensively on the Eastern Front and provided the division with a versatile, comparatively mobile base of fire. Although these howitzers delivered armour-piercing and shaped-charge anti-tank rounds, they were far from being effective anti-tank weapons. The artillery regiments were given the primary tasks of destroying enemy positions and fortified defences, and conducting counter-battery fire prior to an armoured or infantry assault.

A 2cm quadruple flak gun mounted on a halftrack. The flak gunner can be seen surveying the sky using a pair of 6 × 30 binoculars. These lighter calibre guns were much respected by Soviet aircrews and were also devastating against light vehicles, as well as soldiers caught out in the open.

A photograph showing two Sd.Kfz.10/4 halftracks mounting the 2cm FlaK 30 gun. Note the second halftrack is towing the Sd.Ah.51 trailer. The column's advance has taken the vehicles through a town destroyed by intensive fighting.

Mounted on a cruciform platform is an 8.8cm flak gun positioned in a destroyed town. The 8.8cm flak gun barrel is in a horizontal position indicating that it is being used against a ground target. Note the Luftwaffe flak crew preparing their gun for a possible fire fight.

Wehrmacht anti-tank gunners preparing to use their PaK 35/36 anti-tank gun. This weapon was the first anti-tank gun mass produced and saw service in both the Wehrmacht and Waffen-SS until the end of the war. Even by 1941, when this weapon first made its debut on the Eastern Front, German gunners soon realized how limited the weapon was in an anti-tank role. In spite of this the weapon still saw extensive action during the last years of the war including many defensive actions in the Baltic states.

(*Above*) A sIG 15cm artillery crew preparing their weapon for a fire mission in the snow against an enemy position. This infantry gun was a reliable and robust weapon and was used extensively by the Waffen-SS until the end of the war. A typical infantry regiment controlled three infantry battalions, an infantry gun company with six 7.5cm le.IG 18 guns, two 15cm sIG 33 guns, and an anti-tank company with twelve 3.7cm PaK 35/36 guns. The 15cm sIG 33 infantry gun was regarded as the workhorse piece operated by specially trained infantrymen.

(*Opposite above*) Luftwaffe field troops dressed in distinctive Wehrmacht splinter colours in a trench somewhere in Army Group North. During the war the Luftwaffe units saw extensive action fighting in a dual-purpose role, both on the ground and in the air. It was not until later in 1942, when the German armies were suffering great losses, that Hitler decided to raise Luftwaffe Field Divisions in order to bolster the dwindling forces in the East. The Luftwaffe Field Divisions initially remained under Luftwaffe command, but late in 1943 those that had not already been disbanded were handed over to the army and were reorganized as standard infantry divisions.

(*Opposite below*) Wehrmacht troops are being carried to the forward edge of the battlefield by Sd.Kfz.251 halftracks. This was often the quickest way to dispatch soldiers to support or bolster the front lines.

(*Above*) Waffen-SS troops supported by a light MG 34 machine gunner and his team are seen taking cover along an earth mount along a road. When times and conditions allowed, machine gun crews invariably prepared a number of fallback positions. They appreciated the full value of the MG 34, and along these fallback positions the machine gunners were able to set up advantageous defensive positions. In the face of the mighty Soviet Army time and time again SS units stood firm against almost impossible odds. Even some of the most fanatical SS troops fighting in the Baltic states must have realized that military success was now impossible, yet they continued to make sacrifice after sacrifice, often holding the lines with a few MG 34 and MG 42 machine gun positions in order to allow other units to withdraw.

(*Opposite above*) Waffen-SS troops loading a 15cm Nebelwerfer 41 for a fire mission. This weapon fired 2.5kg shells from a six-tube mounted rocket launcher to a maximum range of 7,000 metres. When fired the projectiles screamed through the air terrifying the enemy with the noise. They were handled by independent army rocket launcher battalions and caused extensive carnage in enemy lines.

(*Opposite below*) A Soviet mortar crew in action against a German position during heavy fighting in Army Group North. It was common for infantry during periods of action to fire their mortar from either trenches or dug-in positions where the mortar could be protected by enemy fire.

(*Right*) A Waffen-SS MG 42 machine gun crew wade across muddy terrain. Although along many sectors of Army Group North the German front fought with fanatical resistance and held in a number of places, it came with a high price in men and materials. The German soldier was capable of meeting the highest standards, fighting courageously with self-sacrifice against massive numerical superiority.

(*Opposite above*) A 10.5cm artillery gunner plugs his ears and the artillery piece is fired. The 10.5cm howitzer had a nine-man crew. Unusually fewer are seen serving this piece because often some of the crew were to the rear with the horses, limber and caisson. The 10.5cm light field howitzer was used extensively in the East and provided the division with a versatile, comparatively mobile base of fire. Although these howitzers fielded armour-piercing and shaped-charge anti-tank rounds, they were not effective anti-tank weapons.

(*Opposite below*) An Sd.Kfz.251 halftrack advances along a road bound for the front lines. The Sd.Kfz.251 became one of the most popular halftracks used during the war not only to carry troops into battle but also to tow ordnance and stow other important equipment. It was primarily the success of the Sd.Kfz.251 in the early war years that afforded halftracks a frontline combat role alongside the Panzer on the Eastern Front.

Positioned inside a shelter is a 10.5cm howitzer along with gun crew. In this case the gun is positioned inside a shelter, with probably no support facilities at the rear. Such shelters offered no real protection from enemy fire, but did protect the gun, ammunition, and crew from the rain, and provided a degree of concealment.

A lull on the front lines and artillery men belonging to an unidentified 15cm field howitzer battery rest. The 15cm howitzers are seen in their horizontal position. This particular gun was primarily designed to attack targets deeper in the enemy's rear. This included command posts, reserve units, assembly areas, and logistics facilities.

A Soviet soldier armed with the famous 7.62 Ruchnoy Pulemyot DP Light Machine Gun during an attack against German positions.

The crew of a 15cm sIG 33 infantry gun prepare their weapon for a fire mission in the snow. While the sIG 33 was a reliable and robust weapon, it was rather heavy for an infantry gun. Nonetheless it was used with great success, especially during the early part of the war in Russia.

(*Opposite above*) Soldiers wearing their white reversible camouflage suits can be seen with a whitewashed Marder II tank destroyer. One of the main problems with the Marder on the battlefield was survivability. The combination of a high silhouette and open-top fighting compartment made them vulnerable to artillery fire, low flying aircraft, and grenades. Their armour was also quite thin.

(*Opposite below*) Grenadiers taking shelter inside a wooded area in Army Group North during winter operations. The soldiers are wearing their two-piece snowsuits with whitewashed M35 helmets and toques. These snowsuits provided good freedom of movement for the troops, especially while skiing. The men are wearing the standard equipment for a rifleman with the usual belt and cartridge pouches, which were generally not camouflaged.

(*Above*) A photograph taken the moment a PaK gun is fired in anger against an enemy position inside a Soviet town during intensive fighting in Army Group North.

A German PaK 97/38 gunner with a pair of 6 × 30 Zeiss binoculars in a position overlooking a wooded area. Along the edge of the trees is a knocked-out T-34 Soviet tank. Note the log cabin being built.

A halftrack moves along a road in the snow towing an 8.8cm flak gun. The 8.8cm flak gun was a deadly and effective piece of weaponry which scored numerous hits in anti-aircraft fighting and against ground targets as well.

Chapter Three

The Crushing of Vilnius

Throughout May and June 1944, the Narva Front continued to hold as the Russians built up their reserves for a new offensive. The Germans too were attempting to bring additional reinforcements to the area in order to try to contain themselves cohesively on the battlefield. Although the temporary lull had given the Germans time to build a number of new defensive positions, Army Group North were now exposed by an even greater menace that would threaten Lithuania. On 22 June 1944, the Russians unleashed their long-awaited summer offensive in Army Group Centre, codenamed Operation Bagration. Within a matter of weeks seventeen German divisions had been destroyed. The Soviet attack was so swift that by early July the 1st Baltic Front was now driving towards Baranovichi and then Molodechno and onto Vilnius, the capital of the Baltic state of Lithuania.

By 7 July Baranovichi was finally captured and the focus of effort immediately shifted to the north for Vilnius. The Russians attacked towards Slonim and Vilnius and widened the deployment of their forces, especially against German blocking units. However, German forces in the area were not going to give up ground that easily. On the Baranovichi–Berezovka road heavy fighting broke out as parts of the 4th Panzer Division halted and tried to contain Red Army units moving west along the road. The 507th Heavy Tank Battalion counter-attacked at Leipciani and what followed was a brutal tank battle between the battalion's Tigers and the enemy. After the successful engagement the battalion withdrew east of the Berezovka forest which enabled the Soviets to advance at breakneck speed towards Vilnius.

Already the Soviet 5th Guards Tank Army had bypassed the 5th Panzer Division which was attempting to reach the city. Vilnius was under Hitler's 'Fortified Area' order and the Führer had made it perfectly clear to his commanders that it must be held at all costs. Hitler was hoping to defend the city with four Panzer divisions but was told these could not be assembled before 23 July. It was imperative to hold Vilnius, he said, because without the city it would become a springboard for the Russians to carve their way through Lithuania onto the Baltic Sea shores and then into East Prussia. Without the city he was concerned that it would become almost impossible to re-establish a sustainable connection between the two German army groups.

The fortress of Vilnius was under the command of Luftwaffe General Rainer Stahel, and elements of the 3rd Panzer Army under the command of General Reinhardt. Over the next few days the German garrison at Vilnius tried to hold out against heavy attacks from the 5th Guards Tank Army. During the night of 10 to 11 July Luftwaffe combat formations with 8.8cm flak guns were committed in the fortress of Vilnius and reported that they had successfully destroyed thirty enemy tanks. During the course of twenty-four hours the Luftwaffe managed a number of successful engagements against the enemy, but the situation had drastically deteriorated and it soon became clear that the fortress could no longer hold. In spite of the appalling conditions and the chaotic nature of the situation the defenders continued to resist enemy attacks for as long as possible. With the position deteriorating by the hour, General Stahel proposed to break out west during the night of 12/13 July. After destroying all their heavy weapons, they broke out of the city in a westerly direction. Almost 3,000 soldiers in total left Vilnius, with many frantically swimming the river to reach lead elements of the 6th Panzer Division.

Over the next forty-eight hours, Russian infantry began driving back the remaining German defenders into the city and began to pulverize it street by street. Heavily clad grenadiers resisted well but strong Red Army units managed to split the German garrison defending the city into two pockets. Isolated units spent hours fighting a bloody defence in the ruins. Russian soldiers frequently requested them to surrender, but the Germans preferred to die fighting than capitulate to their Red foe. As the Russians intensified the bombing of the city it soon became apparent that the fortress could no longer withstand enemy fire and the fate of the defenders trapped inside was sealed. Altogether, some 13,000 German troops had been killed or wounded in the defence of Vilnius, and what remained of the garrison capitulated after more than five days of continuous combat.

(*Opposite above*) Out in the snow during winter operations in 1943. In front of their commander soldiers are wearing the winter reversible suit with the white side outermost. This garment consisted of hooded jacket, trousers and mittens. The material used for the uniform was padded insulating material with water-repellent fabric outer shell. Note how discoloured the white material has become with grime and dirt.

(*Opposite below*) In the snow are a number of armoured vehicles: an Sd.Kfz.251 halftrack, a Panther, and a Pz.Kpfw.IV (*Panzerkampfwagen*). The Pz.Kpfw.IV became the most popular Panzer in the *Panzerwaffe* and remained in production throughout the war. Originally the Pz.Kpfw.IV was designed as an infantry support tank, but soon proved to be so versatile and effective that it earned a unique offensive and defensive role on the battlefield.

(*Above*) A column of Panther tanks during combat operations in Russia during the winter months. The first Panthers were produced in January 1943, and by the end of the month were already being distributed to the units for training. However, due to mechanical problems, most were returned to the factories for a major rebuild. Even by the time they saw operations in the summer of 1943, further mechanical problems were found. Following extensive overhaul they were once again returned to their units for operational duties, and by the beginning of 1944 they were embroiled in major defensive and offensive fighting where they fought exceptionally in all theatres of combat.

(*Opposite above*) Luftwaffe field *truppen* converse during winter operations in 1943. By the beginning of 1943 the Luftwaffe field divisions and corps were already employed on various sectors of the Eastern Front and were embroiled in some fierce fighting. Although the Luftwaffe field units saw extensive action, their success was limited and localized and did little to avert enemy operations.

(*Opposite below*) Specially adapted flatbed railway cars have halted at a railway siding and support vehicles are disembarking. Utilizing the railway network, while involving a high risk from enemy aerial attacks, proved efficient at moving units and sometimes whole divisions quickly to the forward edge of the battlefield.

(*Above*) Troops can be seen with a knocked-out Soviet T-34 tank. The men are all wearing their white snow suits. Note the coloured arm bands on their upper arms. With Red Army soldiers wearing similar winter clothing, frontline German troops were normally issued with these coloured armbands which enabled them to distinguish between friend and foe.

(*Opposite above*) Driving across an icy stream a halftrack prime mover can be seen towing a PaK gun. The performance of the German Army on the battlefield was attributed in large part to the halftrack that transported troops, ordnance and supplies to the front. These front-wheel steering vehicles with tracked drive transformed the fighting ability of both the Wehrmacht and Waffen-SS during the Second World War.

(*Opposite below*) Advancing across the snow are Wehrmacht troops being supported by a Tiger tank. The men wear the green splinter pattern Army camouflage smocks. As with most of the later version winter camouflage smocks these uniforms proved to be extremely comfortable and as a combat garment gave the wearer plenty of freedom of movement and at the same time plenty of concealment. Note the radio operator with the radio set attached to his back.

(*Left*) A Panther tank negotiates its way through a town in northern Russia watched by what appears to be an armed motorcycle rider. He is wearing the standard motorcycle waterproof coat. Motorcyclists could be found in every unit of an infantry and Panzer division, especially during the early part of the war. They were even incorporated in the divisional staffs, which included a motorcycle messenger platoon.

(*Opposite above*) During combat, German rifle troops wear their winter smocks complete with personal equipment. Attached to the support straps, they are wearing the gas mask canister, canteen, bread bag, and ammunition pouches for the 98K rifle. Out in the distance Tiger tanks can be seen moving forward.

(*Opposite below*) The crew of a 7.5cm PaK 40 position their gun for firing during the winter of 1943. In service this anti-tank weapon proved powerful and deadly and became the most widely used German anti-tank gun between 1942 and 1944. Note the white sheet wrapped around the barrel in order to break up its distinctive shape in the snow.

(*Above*) An assault gun has become stuck in muddy water and a halftrack is attempting to pull the stricken vehicle out using the StuG's tow cables. The origins of the assault guns, or *Sturmgeschütz*, initially lay in German artillery demands for an armoured vehicle that had armour-piercing and high explosive capabilities and could provide instant attacking infantry fire support. In spite of the StuG's proven tank-killing potential and its service on the battlefield both in offensive and defensive roles, the increased use of the StuG as an anti-tank weapon began depriving the infantry of the fire support for which the assault gun was originally built.

(*Opposite above*) An Ausf.G variant rolls along a road. The crew have expertly applied foliage over the vehicle for camouflage while driving during daylight hours. Note there is only one piece of side skirt left on the right side.

(*Opposite below*) Riflemen and MG 34 gun crews advance through a captured Russian town. A Pz.Kpfw.IV is supporting this advanced column as it makes its way through to the front.

A photograph showing a shelter or *Halbgruppenunterstand* (half-group living bunker). Note the inscription 'Melder' above the entrance to the bunker. Translated this means messenger or runner. This bunker is probably a forward observation position.

In a *Halbgruppenunterstand* troops can be seen wearing the standard German Army issue greatcoat and matt finish M35 steel helmets. By late 1943 enemy aerial bombing along Army Group North became so perilous in certain sectors that German units spent almost the whole day hiding underground or in makeshift shelters.

German troops advance across a railway line during operations in 1943. The unit's commander converses with another soldier who is obviously standing on one of the railway goods wagons.

Gebirgsjäger or mountain troops have disembarked at a railway siding and are unloading supplies and horses. Even during the last two years of the war, contrary to popular belief, the main motive power of the German Army was still the horse. Millions of these hapless animals were killed on the Eastern Front alone.

During a ceremony, soldiers are being decorated for their bravery in the field. The soldiers are wearing the M1943 field cap. This field cap became the most popular item of headgear worn by the German Army from 1943 onwards.

Russian soldiers can be seen advancing through a town during winter operations in the late winter of 1943.

Two Sd. Kfz.251 armoured personnel carriers have halted on a road with well-armed Panzergrenadiers ready to dismount at a moment's notice. For the troops this was the most effective and quickest way of being transported either to the battlefield, or being withdrawn to another line of defence. When the halftracks arrived at the edge of a battlefield, the troops were able quickly to dismount and take up positions.

(*Above*) In a destroyed Russian town, signalmen can be seen crossing a road. Note the soldier carrying the cable on a reel connected to his back on a special frame. This signals soldier was nicknamed the 'line puller' or *Strippenzieher*. Often the cables were connected on poles to a radio truck (*Funkkraftwagen*). For speed on the battlefield, signalmen frequently laid cables on the ground, as in this photograph, but this way the cables were susceptible to breakages from passing traffic running over them.

(*Opposite page*) Two photographs showing a gun crew with their 7.5cm PaK 40. In a defensive stronghold a typical German line comprised mainly of light and heavy MG 34 and MG 42 machine guns, an anti-tank rifle company or battalion, a sapper platoon that was equipped with a host of various explosives, infantry guns, an anti-tank artillery company which had a number of anti-tank guns, and occasionally a self-propelled gun.

(*Left*) German troops on the march passing a knocked-out Soviet T-34 tank. An MG 34 machine gunner can be seen with his weapon slung over his shoulder. The vast majority of distances travelled in Russia were on foot. This was sometimes debilitating for the soldiers, especially when they were also compelled to fight.

(*Opposite page*) The crew of an Sd.Kfz.251 during a routine stop can be seen next to a building and some trees. Some of the crew's undergarments are seen hanging out to dry on a line between two trees. Note the M35 steel helmets attached to the side of the vehicle.

(*Below*) An excellent view of a column of StuGs halted along a road. In 1943 the StuG had become a very popular assault gun, especially on the Eastern Front. Its low profile and mechanical reliability saw their employment grow on the battlefield. Over 3,000 of them were operational in 1943. Due to their popularity, from 1943 until the end of the war the assault guns were slowly absorbed into the Panzer units and Panzer grenadier divisions of the Wehrmacht and Waffen-SS.

(*Above*) In a forward observation post a soldier can be seen looking through a pair of scissor binoculars. The observer was primarily tasked with detecting targets and looked for weapon muzzles, moving infantry, armoured vehicles, fires, smoke from cooking and anything else that might help them locate their enemy. From this position he could send details of enemy movements back to divisional headquarters.

(*Opposite above*) Soviet troops on the march through a town. During the summer of 1943 the German front continued to hold. Both the Germans and Soviets in northern Russia were almost equal in active-duty strength. German strength in July was 710,000 men and Army Group North was building up a huge number of reserves echeloned in depth behind the northern fronts in Estonia and Latvia. The Red Army was also known to have substantial reserves and was building up significant forces to weaken Army Group North's defensive positions around Leningrad and Nevel.

(*Opposite below*) Russian soldiers with armoured support charge into action in this Soviet propaganda photograph.

(*Right*) An armed Soviet soldier receives a group of German troops from an unidentified unit belonging to 18th Army that have surrendered. By the end of 1943 Army Group North's tactical position had become very fragile in a number of places. This was made worse on 14 January 1944 when the Red Army launched its winter offensive against the Leningrad and Volkhov Fronts. The German 18th Army was outnumbered by at least 3:1 in divisions, 3:1 in artillery, and 6:1 in tanks, self-propelled artillery, and aircraft.

(*Opposite page*) Tank commanders converse with the aid of maps. Behind them is a whitewashed Pz.Kpfw.IV tank. The vehicle looks like it's been embroiled in some heavy enemy contact as most of its side skirts are missing.

(*Below*) An Sd.Kfz.251 halftrack advances along a sandy road toward stationary Panzers during the summer of 1943.

(*Above*) Panzer grenadiers can be seen out in a snow-covered field. In the field a knocked-out Pz.Kpfw.IV can be seen with a missing track on its left side, probably due to a mine. The tank still retains its summer camouflage scheme.

(*Opposite page*) A photograph taken during winter operations in 1943/44 of a whitewashed Nashorn tank destroyer. The Nashorn was issued to the heavy anti-tank battalions (*schwere Panzerjäger-Abteilungen*). The Nashorn's gun was a variant of the PaK 43, one of the most effective anti-tank guns deployed during the war.

(*Above*) Heavily-armed Panzergrenadiers with their deadly *Panzerfäuste* slung over their shoulders trudge forward along a road in support of a column of Jagdpanzer IV. During 1944 both tank-destroyers and assault guns gradually outnumbered the tanks in the field, which was confirmation of the Panzerwaffe's obligation to perform a defensive role against overwhelming opposition. All of these vehicles became irrevocably stretched along a very thin Eastern Front with few of them ever reaching the proper operating level. Panzer divisions too were often broken up and split among hastily constructed battle groups drawn from a motley collection of armoured formations. But still these battle groups were put into the line operating well below strength.

(*Opposite above*) Troops cross what appears to be a destroyed wooden bridge. They are armed with their standard 98K rifle and wear the waterproof *Zeltbahn* which was carried by each German soldier as part of his personal equipment. The Zeltbahn could be worn as a poncho over the field equipment, and it could also be worn buttoned up under the equipment as a form of camouflage.

(*Opposite below*) A Nashorn tank destroyer loaded onboard a special railway flat-car bound for the front in the winter of 1944. In spite the terrible setbacks on the Eastern Front, the Panzerwaffe continued to prove its worth on the battlefield. In order to increase the strength of the Panzerwaffe in the East a variety of modified tanks were produced including the Nashorn, which mounted the powerful self-propelled 8.8cm PaK 43/1.

A whitewashed Tiger tank in Russia during winter combat. Panzergrenadiers are being supported by the tank, giving them protection from frontal enemy fire.

Inside a wooded area, a late variant whitewashed Pz.Kpfw.IV navigates through the undergrowth under the instruction of a Panzergrenadier. Note that a number of other Panzergrenadiers have hitched a lift on board the tank. These men could dismount at a moment's notice to go into action or take cover from enemy aerial or ground attack.

One of the most popular armoured vehicles supporting ground combat during the latter part of the war was the StuG III. In this photograph this late variant StuG III Ausf.G has halted in a village. Note on the front armoured plates smoke candle dischargers, and spare track links have been bolted to the vehicle for additional armoured protection.

Troops repairing their Sd.Kfz.250 halftrack in a snowy wood. This vehicle was used in a variety of roles on the battlefield, very similar to the Sd.Kfz.251. Unlike its larger cousin, this halftrack version was a basic troop carrier and was used as an armoured personnel carrier for reconnaissance units, carrying scout sections.

(*Opposite page*) Waffen-SS troops belonging to the 4SS Panzergrenadier 'Polizei' Division. The soldiers have dug a slit trench in a wooded area affording them concealment against both aerial and ground detection. This is more than likely a forward observation post. Note a number of commanders conversing with their men. In the winter of 1943, the division saw action south of Lake Ladoga, but due to vicious and unceasing attacks it was reluctantly forced to withdraw to a new defensive line at Kolpino where it was successful in holding the Red Army, despite suffering heavy casualties.

(*Above*) Waffen-SS combat troops at Narva dishevelled and exhausted. Although the Russians won the battle of Narva in the winter of 1944, the Germans had in fact delayed the enemy advance for a number of months and inflicted terrible damage on their forces. The first half of 1944 had been a period of disasters for the German armies on the Eastern Front, but Hitler had good reason to be pleased with the performance of his Waffen-SS divisions. They had shown courage in the face of overwhelming strength and stood firm against almost impossible odds. Narva was a battle that stood as an example in which the SS made sacrifice after sacrifice, often holding the line to allow other units to escape. Few other units could engender such confidence from their Führer. But the Waffen-SS were not supermen, and their time would come when ultimately they would not be able to stave off defeat.

Chapter Four

Withdrawal

Along the German Baltic front the Germans were experiencing defensive problems in many areas and in spite of strong fortified positions manned with
PaK (*Panzerabwehrkanone*) guns and lines of machine gun pits. The Red Army
moved forward in their hundreds regardless of the cost in life to their own ranks.
All along the battered and blasted front German troops tried in vain to hold their
positions against overwhelming odds. While parts of the German line simply cracked
under the weight of the Russian onslaught, there were numerous areas where
German units continued to demonstrate their ability to defend the most unpromising
positions against well-prepared and superior enemy forces. Along the Narva Front
German infantry divisions bitterly contested large areas of countryside. Fighting was
often savage, resulting in terrible casualties on both sides.

In spite Germany's dogged resistance to hold its lines, the decimation of Army
Group Centre meant that much of the pressure now fell on Army Group North. By
mid-July the Red Army had already taken full advantage of the situation and was
slowly grinding down German forces in both Estonia and Lithuania. In order to avert a
catastrophe a new defensive line was built called the Tannenberg Line (*Tannen-
bergstellung*) with the main defences erected to the west of Narva. On 21 July Hitler
grudgingly ordered his forces to withdraw to the Tannenberg Line, and from there
fight to the death.

Three days later, on 24 July, strong Russian forces attacked the Tannenberg Line.
What followed was a series of bloody infantry and armoured battles that saw the
Germans dwarfed by enemy superiority. Both German and Estonian forces tried to
hold their defensive positions, but in many places were pulverized by the 2,000 tons
of shells and grenades thrown at them. The Red Army attack engulfed much of the
front, but this did not deter German and Estonian frontline troops accompanied by
Panther tanks and rocket artillery from launching a series of savage counter-attacks of
their own. Some of the counter-attacks were so fierce that the Germans managed to
recapture the towns of Tornimägi and Grenaderimägi.

During the morning of 25 July, as troops on the Tannenberg Line fought for
survival, 1,360 Soviet assault guns fired nearly 300,000 shells and grenades as the
Second Shock Army began attacking across the Narva River. The remaining Estonian

defensive positions that had not been blasted by the shelling were attacked and in many areas these last strongpoints ran out of ammunition. As the Estonian troops fled in panic they were cut down by Russian fire. Along the banks of the Narva both German and Estonian Wehrmacht and Waffen-SS forces were driven from their trenches and foxholes. As confusion swept across the entire front commanders in the field hastily gathered the remaining units together to try to defend the main highway to Tallinn. The situation for the defenders was calamitous. The Germans were well aware how important it was to prevent the Russians advancing on Tallinn, but there seemed no stopping the Red Army drive.

During late July the Germans fought a number of triumphant defensive actions trying in vain to hold the Soviets from pushing along the Tallinn highway. Although the German withdrawal to the Tannenberg Line was reached successfully by many retreating units, the city of Narva could no longer be held and as a consequence the Russians finally captured it after six long months of battle which had cost the lives of nearly 500,000 men.

In the first week of August the German position in Estonia and Latvia looked increasingly grim. Army Group North were exhausted and the Russians were relentlessly driving them back by pouring troops, often boy soldiers and old men, at every weak point along the receding front.

On 10 August the Third Baltic and Second Baltic Fronts launched massive air and artillery attacks against the 18th Army south of Pskov Lake and north of the Dvina. The attacks were fierce and within only a few days, holes were punched through the German lines bringing fear that Estonia would soon be lost. Thousands of Germans troops were killed or wounded trying to hold back the attacks. Those that were left to defend Estonia were exhausted and much reduced in numbers. In a radical effort to prevent the front from caving in, General Heinz Guderian, Chief of the General staff, proposed that thirty divisions of Army Group North, which were redundant in Kurland, be shipped back to the Reich so they could be resupplied and brought up to strength, and from there sent to reinforce Army Group Centre in Poland. Hitler, however, emphatically refused Guderian's proposal. Kurland and the Estonian islands of Hiiumaa and Saaremaa were to hold out, he said. This, he believed, was necessary to protect German U-boat bases along the Baltic coast.

While preparations were made for the defence of Kurland and the Estonian islands, on 17 September, General Ferdinand Schörner, commander of Army Group North, decided to evacuate his forces from Estonia before they were driven along the Baltic coast and cut off. The withdrawal was codenamed Operation Aster. It began with evacuating elements of the German formations and Estonian civilians. In less than a week some 50,000 troops and 1,000 PoWs had been removed. The remaining parts of Army Group North in Estonia were ordered to withdraw into Latvia through the town of Pärnu. As German forces retreated, the infantry were ground down in a battle of attrition and could no longer sustain itself cohesively on the battlefield. The Russians advanced towards Tallinn in overwhelming superiority across the flat plains of Estonia using both fields and the long straight highway. Panzergrenadiers, Luftwaffe field units, Waffen-SS and Estonian conscripts tried in vain to hold back the enemy onslaught.

By 22 September Tallinn was captured and two days later the Red Army bombed Vormsi Island and the harbour at Haapsalu preventing desperate German units from escaping by sea. The Russian 8th Army of the Leningrad Front then went on to capture the remaining islands off the Estonian coast in amphibious attacks.

A staff car pulls alongside a StuG III Ausf.G. The vehicle carries the square pennant associated with a divisional commander and a triangle-shaped pennant of an Army or Army Group commander.

(*Above*) A Panther tank halted next to a house during winter combat. Note that foliage including branches from a tree have been applied to the front armoured plates of the vehicle in order to break up the tank's distinctive shape.

(*Opposite page*) An elevated 8.8cm flak gun during a fire mission against an enemy aerial target. This gun is part of a battery of flak guns. The 8.8cm flak gun performed very well in its original role of anti-aircraft gun and it proved to be a superb anti-tank gun as well. As the war in the East raged on, many of these guns were transferred from air defence units to anti-tank duties.

(*Right*) One of the most impressive mortars used by both the Wehrmacht and Waffen-SS on the Eastern Front was the 12cm Granatwerfer 378(r), as seen here being readied for fire by a Wehrmacht mortar crew. The weapon consisted of a circular base plate, the tube and the supporting bipod, and weighed 285kg. Because of its weight, a two-wheeled axle was utilized, enabling the mortar to be towed into action. The axle could be quickly removed before firing. The weapon fired the Wurfgranate 42 round, which contained 3.1kg of explosives.

(*Above*) Two commanders in the field converse standing next to an Sd.kfz.250 during winter operations. In front of the halftrack is a halted whitewashed Pz.Kpfw.IV with intact side skirts.

(*Opposite page*) Out in the field is an assault gunner on his field telephone. Behind him is a stationary Hummel assault vehicle. Note the letter 'G' painted on the rear indicating that it is the 7th gun in the battery.

(*Below*) Across a frozen plain are a number of armoured vehicles during a fire mission. In the distance, Sd.Kfz.251 halftracks can be seen advancing. A Panther tank can also be identified, along with a Pz.Kpfw.IV.

An MG 42 light machine gunner marching with his troop across a snowy field. Although a machine gun troop was normally a three-man squad, due to the high casualty rates suffered on the Eastern Front they were commonly reduced to two; but they were still highly effective.

An Sd.Kfz.10 halftrack mounting a 5cm flak gun has halted in the snow. Its crew is preparing a position next to the vehicle. Digging in such conditions must have been extremely difficult with the ground so frozen. Often troops lit fires in order to soften the ground, but it was risky as smoke from a fire could give away a position.

A command Sd.Kfz.251 halftrack with radio antennae frame halts next to another Sd.Kfz.251. The commander wearing a sheepskin coat can be seen conversing with the command vehicle. Both vehicles are armed with the mounted MG 34 machine gun and splinter shield for local defence.

Troops wearing their two-piece winter suits are preparing to move out for combat duties. The troops are mainly armed with the standard 98K carbine infantry rifle, but there is a soldier armed with a captured Russian PPSh-41 sub-machine gun.

Troops prepare to move out from their position. In 1944 Army Group North had been ground down through a battle of attrition and as a consequence could no longer sustain itself cohesively on the battlefield. For months the Army Group had fought desperately to maintain unity and hold their positions in the north, fighting for which often saw thousands of soldiers perish. It now not only lacked sufficient weapons and equipment, but was also short of manpower.

Out in the snow an 8.8cm flak gun can be seen being used in an anti-tank role. The dismounted limber can be seen next to the flak gun as a precautionary measure in case the crew needed to hastily reposition the gun.

A ski patrol belonging to SS Gebirgs-Division 'Nord' on patrol. They all wear the two-piece snow suit (*Schneeanzug*). Operations in the winter were often brutal for the men fighting and proper shelter was frequently at a premium.

A commanding officer converses with his men. They are wearing a variety of different kits. Three of the soldiers are wearing the standard two-piece Wehrmacht splinter reversible garment and one is wearing it white-side out. Note his grey M35 steel helmet, which has had streaks of white paint applied to break up its distinctive shape and help camouflage the wearer.

(*Above*) Due to the length of time the front stagnated in the north, troops spent many days and weeks in trenches. In this photograph, soldiers pose for the camera in one of these trenches. Their position has been partially concealed by a Zeltbahn shelter-quarter. It was very common for infantry, especially during long intensive periods of action, to fight from either trenches or dug-in positions where the men could be protected from enemy fire.

(*Opposite above*) Due to the massive losses sustained by Army Group North, manpower was desperately required to defend the state of Estonia and thus protect the Baltic from the Soviet advance. As a consequence, the Germans ordered the mobilization of 30,000 Latvians and 15,000 Estonians. In this photograph, Estonian troops have been drafted into the German Army to defend their land from the Russian attack.

(*Opposite below*) An interesting photograph showing Estonian troops, also known as the Estonian Legion, drafted into the German Army holding a Nazi flag during a recruitment action in the city of Tallinn. Two Estonian civilians appear to have just been recruited and are being escorted.

In this photograph, Estonian volunteers are being trained with an MG 42 light machine gun. A commanding officer converses with an Estonian civilian, more than likely running through the training procedure. All across Estonia, border defence regiments, police infantry battalions and other units were formed, together with the Home Guard units, into special German Army Estonian volunteers.

A volunteer recruited into the 3rd Estonian SS brigade is decorated in a trench for his bravery in the field. Some 7,000 soldiers had been drafted into two SS battalion regiments that once formed the Estonian Legion. By early 1944 these regiments had been renamed as the 20th Waffen Grenadier Division of the SS (1st Estonia).

Newly recruited soldiers of the 20th Waffen Grenadier Division of the SS (1st Estonia) are seen during a ceremony in 1944. Now officially formed as an SS Division the soldiers were forbidden to wear the SS runes on their collars and they began wearing national insignia instead, as seen in this photograph.

Estonian volunteers during a parade ceremony in 1944. The general mobilization for drafting men into the German Army was proclaimed in Estonia on 30 January 1944. Within a year some 50,000 men were mobilized in Estonia to fight for the Germans and defend the Baltic states against the Russians.

Estonian volunteers prepare the defence of the Narva Front in a wooded area. The Soviet attack on Estonia was massive with a force of four armies from the Leningrad front. The German defence was led by Army Group Narva on the Narva front and by the 18th Army on the shores of Lake Peipsi. A number of replenished infantry divisions and other ad hoc troops were drafted to Estonia from other sectors of the front to build up its defences, and were ordered to defend to the death.

Estonian volunteers stand in file in front of their commanding officer, probably holding a morning assembly before being moved out to the front.

Estonian volunteers march through the city of Tallinn in 1944. The defence of Tallinn, by both Army Group North and its Estonian volunteers, was inadequate. This was mainly due to the rapid advance of the Soviet forces smashing through the Narva Front. What was left of Army Group North in Estonia was ordered to withdraw into Latvia through the town of Pärnu. As German forces retreated, the infantry were ground down in a battle of attrition and could no longer sustain itself cohesively on the battlefield. The Russians advanced in overwhelming superiority across the flat plains of Estonia both over fields and using the long straight highway, bound for Tallinn. By 22 September Tallinn was captured.

Estonian troops, wearing the standard Wehrmacht two-piece reversibles splinter side out, wade through under-growth during the defence of Estonia in 1944. For the defence of Estonia the I Battalion, 1st Estonian Regiment was placed at the Yershovo Bridgehead on the east coast of Lake Peipsi. Estonian and German units were ordered to clear the west coast of Lake Peipsi of Soviet forces. As a consequence of this action Russian casualties were counted in their thousands.

Troops stand next to a PaK 40. The 7.5cm PaK 40 was a deadly anti-tank weapon. The gun had a spaced-armour shield which was held together by large bolts. These bolts had drilled holes that allowed the crews to thread foliage through them.

Three photographs showing Estonian volunteers in 1944 during defence of Estonia. The Estonian units were mainly directed under German command and saw extensive action on the Narva line throughout 1944. Many of these Estonia troops were not radical Nazis, and feared Russian occupation of their country. that they would attract support from the Allies, and ultimately a restoration of their interwar independence, by resisting the Soviet reoccupation of their country. In fact, the Germans became so worried about the desperate situation in the Baltics that an agreement had been reached with Estonians, where they were promised amnesty if they chose to fight along in German units, notably the SS.

(*Above*) A bicycle unit prepares to move out. Note the shelter-quarter known as the Zeltbahn being worn by the troops to protect them against rain.

(*Opposite page*) In a trench, soldiers armed with the Mauser 7.9mm Kar 98k carbine, the standard issue shoulder weapon of the Wehrmacht, can be seen in combat. In support of the fighting is a StuG III Ausf.G.

(*Right*) A photograph of a captured Soviet Katyusha multiple rocket launcher for which German troops coined the nickname 'Stalin's organ' (*Stalinorgel*). These rocket launchers were much feared by the Germans, and the devastation they caused to the front lines was immense.

(*Opposite above*) German troops rest in a field. In the distance, armoured vehicles comprising Pz.Kpfw.IVs move forward. Some 812 tanks were deployed on the northern sector of the front during the opening phase of operations on the Eastern Front. However, within a year this amount had significantly been reduced through mechanical breakdowns, wear and tear, growing enemy defensive actions, and armour being shifted south. By 1944, there were fewer than 200.

(*Opposite below*) Panzergrenadiers in slit trenches. In the distance Sd.Kfz.251 armoured personnel carriers can be seen halted in a field.

(*Above*) A Pz.Kpfw.IV advances across a field, followed by an Sd.Kfz.251 armoured personnel carrier. The halftrack has saplings attached, to help conceal it from aerial detection. In 1944 the Soviet Air Force dominated the sky and was frequently attacking German troop concentrations and armoured vehicles, causing severe disruption to movement during the day.

(*Above*) A Volkswagen Type 166 *Schwimmwagen*, which literally means floating/swimming car, seen here in a wooded area. This vehicle was used extensively by both Wehrmacht and Waffen-SS forces and became the most mass-produced amphibious car in history.

(*Opposite above*) A flak crew has utilized their 8.8cm flak gun against a ground target during heavy fighting. During the latter half of the war, as heavier and more lethal Soviet armour was brought to bear against the German Army, German forces clamoured to obtain more flak guns that could deal with the threat of the T-34 tank.

(*Opposite below*) A shirtless flak gunner in his defensive position overlooking a railway line in the early summer of 1944. This flak gun was capable of combating both low-flying aircraft and ground targets.

(*Above*) Wehrmacht troops pose for the camera in front of a captured Soviet T-34 tank that is being used by the Germans on the battlefield. Note the national cross painted on the side of the turret.

(*Opposite above*) From a dugout, an 8cm Gr.W.34 can be seen. During the war the mortar had become the standard infantry support weapon, giving the soldier valuable high-explosive capability beyond the range of rifles or grenades. But it was inaccurate: even with an experienced mortar crew, it generally required ten bombs to achieve one direct hit on a target.

(*Opposite below*) On a motor boat, a group of Wehrmacht soldiers, together with an MG 42 machine gun crew, move across a lake. The MG 42 proved its capabilities in both offensive and defensive actions. Its dependability was second to none and every unit of the German army was equipped with this weapon. By 1944 many units had become totally dependent on them to hold back the attacking enemy.

(*Above*) A Russian defensive position in the Army Group North zone of operations. This soldier is armed with the PPSh machine gun complete with ammunition box. In the field, the PPSh was a durable, low-maintenance weapon that could fire 900 rounds per minute. Some 6 million of them had been produced by the end of the war. The Soviets would often equip regiments and even entire divisions with the weapon, giving them unmatched short-range firepower. The gun had proven such an effective weapon on the battlefield that both the Wehrmacht and Waffen-SS used captured stocks extensively throughout the fighting on the Eastern Front.

(*Opposite page*) A halftrack has halted on a dirt road. Pioneers can be seen preparing the road for vehicles to pass through. Because of the continuous heavy traffic these roads needed constant maintenance.

A quadruple-barrelled self-propelled anti-aircraft gun in a hidden position in a field. By 1944, mechanized formations were well equipped with flak guns. There were motorized flak battalions, with divisions being furnished with additional anti-aircraft platoons and companies in the Panzergrenadier, Panzer and artillery regiments. This flak gun was a formidable weapon and was more than capable of combating both low flying aircraft and ground targets.

Young Estonian flak volunteers stand to attention in front of Luftwaffe officers during a passing out ceremony in 1944.

On a railway platform, Estonian volunteers are seen wearing German standard issue Wehrmacht greatcoats and M1938 field caps. These new recruits appear to be at a ceremony before leaving for the front. It is probable that the civilians in the photograph are family and loved ones and local dignitaries.

A Latvian mortar crew in action against a Soviet target during winter operations in 1944. By the end of 1944 the German front lines were now badly scarred and depleted, and the bulk of its forces no longer had sufficient supplies or manpower to maintain its positions. German troops, together with Latvian and Estonian volunteers, battered and bruised from months of ceaseless combat were desperately trying to hold their positions, but the situation had deteriorated far quicker than the German high command had anticipated.

(*Right*) Waffen-SS officers converse during operations in Estonia in 1944. It was here in the Baltic states of Estonia, Latvia and Lithuania that German forces and their remaining allied troops tried desperately to prevent the Red Army from spilling across into northern Germany and driving on Berlin.

(*Opposite above*) A 2cm flak gun in action in Estonia in 1944. This weapon was usually served by eight men on a single mount to give a combined cycle rate of fire of 1,800 rounds per minute. The guns also armed a variety of vehicles on self-propelled mounts.

(*Opposite below*) The crew of a Tiger tank rest in a wooded area. The rear of the Tiger can clearly be seen, with its distinctive exhausts. One of the most famous Tiger tanks that fought in the Baltic states belonged to Heavy Tank Battalion (*Schwere Panzer-Abteilung*) 502 in Narva. In January 1944 the tank battalion received 32 replacements, and a further 20 in February 1944, bringing the total strength of sPz.Abt 502 up to seventy-one Tigers on 29 February 1944, although only twenty-four were operational. Despite this, the commander Leutnant Otto Carius led the battalion in a number of successful engagements. The unit fought well around Leningrad and at Narva.

(*Below*) A well camouflaged Sd.Kfz.251 halftrack personnel carrier advances along a dirt road.

(*Right*) An interesting photograph showing a Wehrmacht soldier attaching a rifle grenade to his standard issue 98K rifle. In 1942, an attachable rifle grenade launcher called the *Gewehrgranatengerät* or *Schiessbecher* (shooting cup) was produced. The rifle grenade-propelling cartridges fired a wooden projectile through the barrel to the rifle grenade and upon impact it automatically primed the rifle grenade.

(*Opposite above*) Somewhere along the Baltic coast a German flak gun position is seen in action against an enemy aerial target.

(*Opposite below*) On a muddy road a Volkswagen Type 82 *Kübelwagen* halts next to a track vehicle. This photograph was taken during the winter of 1944.

(*Above*) Waffen-SS troops hitch a lift onboard a halftrack. Even in the Baltic states, where the bulk of the SS were foreign conscripts, Hitler felt he could still rely on these elite units to stave off defeat, or at least hold back the Russian onslaught for a time. However, Hitler's confidence in them was a double-edged sword. The Waffen-SS were constantly rushed from one threatened sector to another and expected to save the front from disaster.

(*Opposite above*) A number of Sd.Kfz.251 halftracks can be seen along with two Pz.Kpfw.IV tanks with intact side skirts. By the winter of 1944/45 the Panzerwaffe was a shadow of its former self. What was left of its armour became loosely organized in ad hoc groups, often piecemeal. In several sectors of the front the remaining tanks and assault guns ran out of fuel and were abandoned by their crews.

(*Opposite below*) A whitewashed halftrack personnel carrier negotiates a shallow river, showing the versatility of this vehicle on the battlefield.

(*Above*) Panzergrenadiers wearing their distinctive winter suits white side out are clearing a path for a column of Pz.Kpfw.IVs.

(*Opposite above*) A halftrack with a mounted 15cm Nebelwerfer rocket launcher.

(*Opposite below*) The crew of a Pz.Kpfw.IV have halted in the snow and rest on top of their vehicle. Panzergrenadiers on foot are supporting the column.

(*Above*) A flak crew with their 8.8cm flak gun during an urbanized fire mission. The gun is clearly being used against ground targets. Note the wicker cases nearby containing the shells. A couple of primed shells sit on top ready to be loaded and fired.

(*Opposite above*) An interesting photograph showing a quadruple flak gun mounted on a cruciform platform out in the snow. Each of these flak guns had a practical rate of fire of 1,200 rounds per minute, with a maximum horizontal range of 4,800 metres. A number of these mounted flak guns were used in the defence of the Baltic states in a desperate attempt to delay the Russian onslaught. However, like so much of the German armour employed in the East, they were too few or dispersed too thinly to make any significant impact on the main Soviet operations which were already capturing or encircling many of the key towns and cities.

(*Opposite below*) Panther tanks have halted along a road. By 1944 Panzers like the Panther had to wage continuous defensive battles in order to wear down the enemy in a war of attrition. During the bitter fighting in Army Group North, the Panther was used extensively. As German troops found themselves constantly becoming either encircled or cut off the Panthers were organized into special rescue units to relieve trapped pockets of Germans. During the course of these daring rescue missions Panther crews fought with tenacity and courage, but time and time again the sheer weight of the Soviet army overwhelmed them. Many Panthers were lost in action as a result of these brave rescue missions, but it was the lack of fuel and ammunition that eventually forced these lethal machines to a standstill.

Chapter Five

End Game

By the end of September 1944, Army Group North was tactically in a more dangerous position than it had ever been before. The front was badly scarred and depleted, the bulk of its forces having withdrawn from Estonia, and it was continually being threatened by attacks in Latvia and Lithuania. German troops, battered and bruised by months of ceaseless combat, desperately tried to hold their positions, but the situation in the Baltic states had deteriorated far quicker than the German high command had anticipated. From Konigsberg in the north the front had been reduced to a coastal strip of some 80 miles in width and over 400 miles in length. In the Tukums-Riga area the 5th Guards Tank Army had broken through to the coast at the end of July and was now threatening the whole area. Infantry units of Army Group North and the 3rd Panzer Army were fighting for survival and were vulnerable everywhere. Hitler was well aware how precarious the situation had become, but was determined not to withdraw his forces out of what had become known as the Tukums-Riga corridor. He told Schörner that Army Group North would have to hold on to northern Latvia against all Soviet attacks. The Red Army were reported to be only 35 miles from Riga on the south and 50 miles from the coast below Lake Vortsjaerv. South of Riga the SS Panzergrenadier Division 'Nordland' dug in along what was known as the Segewold position.

The Red Army's objective was to spearhead the 2nd and 3rd Baltic Fronts on a broad front towards Riga, and as the operation progressed they were to pursue Army Group North into Kurland. Although German commanders in the field were well aware of their enemy's intentions the Germans knew that they were hindered by weak infantry, and lack of armour artillery. In a drastic measure to stabilize the deteriorating situation Schörner began moving divisions through to begin defending the northern tip of Kurland. Reluctantly, and under constant Soviet attacks, the general ordered the withdrawal of his troops from Riga, and two days later the city fell to the 3rd Baltic Front. With the fall of the Latvian capital came the evacuation of thousands of troops and 100,000 tons of material to the Kurland bridgehead. In total some thirty divisions would be moved to the Kurland area where they were ordered to dig in and fight to the death in order to defend what Latvian territory remained in German hands.

The Soviet objective was to crush the German forces in Kurland, where the main body of Army Group North was now positioned. The bulk of these forces consisted of the once much-vaunted German 16th Army and 18th Army. Both armies were given the task of protecting the remaining U-boat forces along the shores of the Baltic by repelling Soviet attacks. Over 500,000 soldiers, including 20,000 men of the Latvian 19th SS-Division, had now evacuated into the Kurland.

The German and Latvian force that was given the task of defending Fortress Kurland was relatively intact and strong, in spite of a lack of tanks, artillery and anti-tank guns. The Germans and their Latvian allies had barely dug into their lines in mid-October when the Soviets attacked. Shells and bullets rained down on the Latvians, but they stood firm. By 22 October the Russians, savagely mauled by the determined defence, fell back. It seemed that the Soviets had underestimated the strength and determination of their enemy. Further attacks on Kurland were unleashed on 27 October, but still the Russians could not breach the outer defences of the Fortress. Soviet commanders were optimistic that it would only be a matter of time before Kurland would be crushed, but they had no idea that this engagement would continue right up until the end of the war.

By late 1944, the Germans had become masters of defence and were expertly dug in. Russian attacks continued with unabated ferocity, but the Germans and Latvians fought bitterly to hold ground. The Red Army tried its best to exploit its air superiority to damage the two main ports and their facilities.

The second battle of the Kurland pocket lasted until 25 November, and although the Germans incurred high casualties it was the Russians that suffered the most. During late November and the first half of December the fighting eased and this allowed the Germans to be resupplied and strengthened, and to evacuate the large numbers of wounded soldiers and civilians back to the Reich.

While the Germans tried their best to bring their defensive positions up to strength, the Soviet Army prepared for the third offensive. The third battle began on 21 December and lasted until New Year's Eve. The Latvians referred to the fighting during this period as the Christmas battles. With at least a six-to-one numerical superiority the Red Army attacked along the front looking for any weak spots for a breakthrough. For hours, Russian aircraft bombed the German and Latvian lines and almost succeeded in cutting though the front near Ventspils. German Grenadiers, however, launched a series of attacks aimed at blunting the Russian drive. Although the Germans suffered high casualties, Red Army losses were far worse.

Over the next few weeks, fighting in Kurland continued with unabated ferocity. By early January 1945, the strength of the German and Latvian force amounted to some 400,000 men. The Red Army was determined as ever to smash Kurland and had collected some sixty divisions in order to prepare its forces for yet another assault. The attack was to coincide with the massive offensive being prepared in the central sector of the Eastern Front against German troops holding the banks of the Vistula in Poland.

On 12/13 January 1945, along the entire 350 miles of the Vistula Front, the German Army was engulfed in a storm of fire. Across snow-covered terrain, Soviet troops and armoured vehicles flooded the battlefield. By the end of the first day the battle had ripped open a breach more than 20 miles wide. The 4th Panzer Army was virtually annihilated.

Simultaneously in Army Group North, Kurland was once again attacked. The Soviet assault was massive, but both the Germans and their Latvian allies fought back with everything they could muster. Just prior to the Red Army assault, Hitler had removed several divisions back to Germany, including Schörner, who had been summoned home to help in the defence of the homeland. He was replaced by General Lothar Rendulic.

Rendulic's force of some twenty-one undermanned divisions had stretched itself even more thinly across the front to cover the lines against Russian attacks, and the Germans were suffering from a lack of provisions. Units were being thrown into battle piecemeal, their commanders hoping that this would stem the enemy's drive through Kurland. To Hitler, Kurland was the last bastion of defence in the East and every soldier, he said, was to stand and fight. As the battles in Kurland continued to intensify and the death toll rose to unprecedented levels, on 25 January Hitler officially renamed Army Group North as Army Group Kurland and formally designated the Kurland region as a Fortress. Hitler made it clear that Army Group Kurland would not be evacuated. He was aware that there was now no possibility of restoring a new land corridor between Kurland and East Prussia. Instead, the force would have to fight to the bitter end as the Red Army commenced the encirclement and slow reduction of the Kurland pocket.

On 12 February 1945, the Red Army once again attacked the Kurland Army, targeting the strategically important port of Libau. For a full month the fifth battle of Kurland raged as the Soviets poured infantry and armoured units into the pocket. The conditions in which the Germans had to fight over the next four weeks were horrific. Some of the more seasoned soldiers had fought at close quarters among the ruins and rubble streets, but never endured a combat of attrition like this. A total of some fifty Russian divisions with nearly 2,400 tanks pulverized the front line around the Kurland pocket. Dozens of *Katyusha* rocket machines fired their fearsome projectiles from their 16-rail launchers miles into enemy lines. Aircraft too mercilessly bombed the pocket and artillery regiments poured a hurricane of fire onto the German positions. The unrelenting attacks wore down the defenders, but once again the Red Army only succeeded in pushing the front back a couple of miles. It was only in the sea where the Soviets caused serious disruption and prevented the bulk of German shipping from entering the port of Libau. Almost all of the U-boats had been chased out of the Baltic; the Germans now had only one operable submarine in the area.

On 17 March the Red Army launched another attack against the fortifications. Many of the defenders, including thousands of Latvian conscripts, believed they were unable to endure another attack, as they were fast running out of the basic supplies necessary to keep them alive. They were also short of ammunition and were relying mainly on animal draught to haul their guns from one battle front to another. All seemed lost, but amazingly, the weary and exhausted troops held out for another few weeks. During this period, the Red Army lost some 70,000 troops and hundreds of tanks trying to break through the pocket. Losses among the Kurland Army too were appalling, yet Hitler remained unyielding in his resolve to abandon the peninsula, in spite of the fact that the Germans were cut off and Russian forces were already advancing through eastern Germany. Hitler decided to relieve the commander of Fortress Kurland, General Lothar Rendulic, and replace him with an even tougher commander, General Carl Hilpert.

For the next three weeks further fighting raged in the pocket, but by early May 1945, when Hitler was dead, plans were made to begin evacuating the last positions in the Kurland that were still fanatically holding out. Although hundreds of ships had already supplied and evacuated the wounded and civilians, there were few ships able to rescue the remaining 200,000 men from Soviet capture. Nevertheless, during the first week of May minesweepers, minelayers, torpedo boats and trawlers ran a shuttle service to carry evacuees from the Kurland harbours and other ports where they could be transferred to larger vessels. All of the ships would risk being sunk from Soviet submarines and aircraft. Every available ship in the eastern Baltic was pressed into service and the vessels were ordered to be loaded to capacity; they would sail for Kiel, Eckernförde and Neustadt. Even when the war was officially declared over, the Russians continued attacking the ships, with some success. It was on 8 May that the last remaining German forces in Kurland capitulated to the Soviets. Hilpert surrendered himself, his personal staff, and three divisions of the XXXVIII Corps to Marshal of the Soviet Union Leonid Govorov. Hilpert sent the following message to his troops:

> To all ranks! Marshall Govorov has agreed to a cease-fire beginning at 14:00 hours on 8 May. Troops to be informed immediately. White flags to be dis-played. Commander expects loyal implementation of order, on which the fate of all Kurland troops depends.

Following the capitulation of the fortress a few days later Russian troops began rounding up the last remaining units that were still determined to fight on to the death. By 11 May the troops of the Leningrad Front had finally secured the Kurland peninsula, reaching the coast of Riga Bay and the Baltic Sea. In total some 140,500 men and non-commissioned officers, 5,083 officers and 28 generals in the Kurland pocket had surrendered. The Russians had also captured 307 tanks and self-propelled guns, 75 aircraft, 1,427 guns, 3,879 machine guns, 52,887 rifles and sub-machine guns, 557 mortars, 219 armoured personnel carriers, 4,281 motor vehicles, 3,442 carts loaded with military equipment, and 14,046 horses.

By 23 May the Soviets had finally completed their round-up of the last remnants of the Kurland Army by which time some 180,000 German troops had been taken into captivity, and with this finally ended the battle of the Baltic and the crushing of Army Group North.

Assault gun crew pose for the camera inside a forest in January 1945 with their whitewashed StuG behind them. For the Panzerwaffe fighting for survival on the Eastern Front shortages of every kind was affecting most of the old and experienced assault gun units. The Soviets had unmatchable material superiority, and yet, despite this major drawback in late 1944 armoured vehicle production, including tanks, assault guns, and self-propelled assault guns, were higher than in any month before May 1944.

(*Opposite above*) Panzergrenadiers on the march pass a stationary Tiger. By early January 1945, the strength of the German and Latvian force amounted to some 400,000 men. The Red Army was determined to smash defensive positions at Kurland, and had collected some sixty divisions in order to prepare its forces for yet another assault on its defences. The attack was to coincide with the massive offensive being prepared in the central sector of the Eastern Front against German troops holding the banks of the Vistula in Poland.

(*Opposite below*) Troops clad in their winter wear on the move being supported by late variant Pz.Kpfw.IVs in the snow. The Germans were suffering from an unmistakable lack of provisions. Many units were simply being thrown into battle as piecemeal, their commanders hoping that it would stem the enemies' drive through Latvia and beyond.

(*Above and following page*) In East Prussia and three photographs show an Sd.Kfz.234/2. This special purpose heavy eight-wheeled armoured car had a crew of four. Its main armament was a 5cm KwK 39/1 L/60. Throughout the war the Germans had realised the success of fast moving, hard hitting wheeled reconnaissance vehicles. This 'Puma', as it was nicknamed, was no exception.

A photograph taken the moment a 10.5cm l.FH18M guns projectile leaves the barrel during defensive action in early 1944. These light field howitzers were constantly modified during the war in order to increase their ranges. Even as the Germans steadily withdrew combat experience soon showed that artillery support was of decisive importance in both defensive and offensive roles. Usually fewer are seen serving this piece because often some of the crew were to the rear with the horses, limber and caisson. The 10.5cm light field howitzer was used extensively in the East and provided the division with a versatile, comparatively mobile base of fire. Although these howitzers provided armour piercing and shaped-charged anti-tank rounds, these guns were far from being effective anti-tank weapons. It was primarily the artillery regiments that were given the task of destroying enemy positions and fortified defences and conducting counter-battery fire prior to an armoured or infantry assault.

(*Opposite above*) An Sd.Kfz.251 armoured personnel carrier with dismounted Panzergrenadiers advance towards the frontline. This was one of the quickest and effective means for troops to enter the forward edge of the battlefield on board a halftrack. By this period of the war there was suicidal opposition from the last remaining SS and Wehrmacht strongpoints which were being grimly held at all costs. Many isolated units spent hours or even days fighting a bloody defence and were slowly ground down by the sheer enemy superiority.

(*Opposite below*) A 5cm PaK 38 (L/60) (5cm *Panzerabwehrkanone* 38 (L/60)) PaK gun on tow being dragged through the snow during operations in Army Group North in the early winter of 1945.

(*Above*) Two photographs showing grenadiers laying the Tellermine 43. These German circular steel cased anti-tank blast mines were laid in their millions on the Eastern Front during the last two years of the war. As the Germans withdrew they laid these mines to help stem the speed of the Soviet advance. The T43 had a unique anti-handling device, and meant that any attempt by the enemy to disarm the mine by unscrewing the pressure plate (to remove the fuse) would automatically trigger detonation.

(*Opposite above*) Troops withdrawing. Everywhere it seemed the Germans were being constantly forced to retreat. Many isolated units spent hours or even days fighting a bloody defence. Russian soldiers frequently requested them to surrender and assured them that no harm would come to them if they did so. But despite this reassuring tone, most German troops continued to fight to the end.

(*Above*) A StuG III advancing along a road in early 1945. The StuG III had been a very popular assault gun on the battlefield. The vehicles had initially provided crucial mobile fire support to the infantry, and also proved their worth as invaluable anti-tank weapon. However, by the early winter of 1944 the StuG was primarily used as an anti-tank weapon, thus depriving the infantry of vital fire support.

(*Opposite below*) Russian forces march westward. For these soldiers it had been a long painful and often very costly march. However, the Red Army were far superior in numbers. The First Byelorussian and First Ukrainian Fronts had the Germans outnumbered on the average by 10:1 in tanks and self-propelled artillery, 9:1 in artillery and troops. In the First Byelorussian Front alone this Russian Army had more infantry, tanks and artillery than the entire German Army on the Eastern Front.

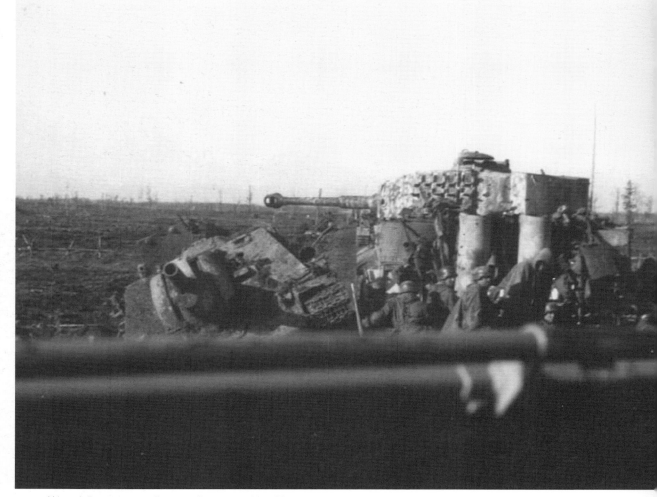

(*Above*) Panzergrenadiers can be seen with a Tiger tank. Next to their position is a knocked out Russian tank. A typical strongpoint deployed along the front comprised of infantry guns, anti-tank artillery company which had a number of anti-tank guns, and occasionally a self-propelled gun. Operating at intervals were Pz.Kpfw.IVs, Tigers, Panthers tanks, and a number of StuG III assault guns, all of which were scraped together. This front-line defensive belt was designated as a killing zone where every possible anti-tank weapon and artillery piece would be used to ambush Soviet tanks.

(*Opposite page*) Scraping the barrel — a newly conscripted *Volkssturm* during the last weeks of the war. Members of the *Volkssturm* only received very basic training and there was also a serious lack of trainers too which meant many of them went to the front barely able to use their weapons properly. The majority of them were armed with either the Karabiner 98K bolt action rifle or the Panzerfaust, but in this photograph the recruit is armed with an MP 38/40 machine gun. It was often down to these men to help defend towns and villages from the onrushing enemy forces. Quite regularly *Volkssturm* conscripts threw down their arms as the attacking forces approached and went into hiding. However, there were some, especially the young, that fought to the death, but still rarely held back the Russian forces for any appreciable time.

An SS defensive position. The troops take a much needed respite and can be seen smoking in one of the many trenches that were dug along the front. These strong points often contained light and heavy MG 34 and MG 42 machine guns, anti-tank rifle company or battalion, a sapper platoon that was equipped with a host of various explosives.

An MG position defending a river crossing confer with their commanding officer. However, whilst it appeared that the Germans were prepared for a Soviet attack, much of the equipment employed along the front was too thinly spread. Commanders too were unable to predict exactly where the strategic focal point of the Soviet attack would take place. To make matters worse when the Russians begun heavily bombing German positions all along the frontier, this also severely weakened the strongest defensive lines.

A Tiger tank crossing through a typical Soviet defensive position of barbed wire entanglements. This was often the first line of defence and was erected to slow advancing foot soldiers before reaching the second line of defence.

Moving to the front StuG III Ausf.Gs have halted to re-fuel. By January/February 1945 the Panzerwaffe was a shadow of its former self. What was left of its armour was now loosely organized in ad hoc groups, often piecemeal. In a number of sectors on the front the remaining tanks and assault guns ran out of fuel and were abandoned by the crew.

Panzergrenadiers rest at the side of the road before resuming their march westward near East Prussia. It was along the borders of East Prussia that the Russians launched their attack on the first parts of the Reich. For the *Volkssturm* and *Hitlerjugend* that were now supporting the Wehrmacht and Waffen-SS, many were going into action for the first time.

Soldiers on the march carrying a variety of arms and provisions to sustain them on the battlefield.

Eight photographs showing grenadiers armed with the deadly *Panzerfaust*. During the last year of the war the *Panzerfaust* was used extensively to combat Russian armour. The *Panzerfaust* consisted of a small, disposable preloaded launch tube firing a high explosive anti-tank warhead, operated by a single soldier. The *Panzerfaust* remained in service in various versions until the end of the war. The weapon often had warnings written in large red letters on the upper rear end of the tube, warning the user of the back blast. After firing, the tube was discarded, making the *Panzerfaust* the first disposable anti-tank weapon.

A column of grenadiers armed with the Karbiner bolt action 98K rifle march westwards in March 1945. On 15 March the Second Belorussian Front opened its final offensive along the Baltic thrusting its powerful force towards the coast at Zoppot between Gotenhafen and Danzig. The Germans tried to defend its positions at all costs, but it was all in vain.

Appendix I

Ranks

German Army	Waffen-SS	British Army
Gemeiner, Landser	Schütze	Private
—	Oberschütze	—
Grenadier	Sturmmann	Lance Corporal
Obergrenadier	—	—
Gefreiter	Rottenführer	Corporal
Obergefreiter	Unterscharführer	—
Stabsgefreiter	—	—
Unteroffizier	Scharführer	Sergeant
Unterfeldwebel	Oberscharführer	Colour Sergeant
Feldwebel	—	—
Oberfeldwebel	Hauptscharführer	Sergeant Major
Stabsfeldwebel	Hauptbereitschaftsleiter	—
—	Sturmscharführer	Warrant Officer
Leutnant	Untersturmführer	Second Lieutenant
Oberleutnant	Obersturmführer	First Lieutenant
Hauptmann	Hauptsturmführer	Captain
Major	Sturmbannführer	Major
Oberstleutnant	Obersturmbannführer	Lieutenant Colonel
Oberst	Standartenführer	Colonel
—	Oberführer	Brigadier General
Generalmajor	Brigadeführer	Major General
Generalleutnant	Gruppenführer	Lieutenant General
General	Obergruppenführer	General
Generaloberst	Oberstgruppenführer	—
Generalfeldmarschall	Reichsführer-SS	—

Appendix II

Order of Battle

Order of Battle, 15 June 1944

THE EASTERN FRONT (UNDER OKH COMMAND)

HEERESGRUPPE 'NORD'

Reserves

12 Panzer Division

SIXTEENTH ARMY

Reserves
24 Infantry Division
69 Infantry Division

281 Security Division
285 Security Division

I Armee Korps

205 Infantry Division

87 Infantry Division

X Armee Korps

389 Infantry Division
290 Infantry Division

263 Infantry Division

II Armee Korps

81 Infantry Division
329 Infantry Division

23 Infantry Division

VI SS Korps

15 SS Grenadier Division 'Latvian 1'
19 SS Grenadier Division 'Latvian 2'

93 Infantry Division

L-Armee Korps

218 Infantry Division
132 Infantry Division

83 Infantry Division

EIGHTEENTH ARMY

Reserves

215 Infantry Division

XXXVIII Armee Korps

21 Luftwaffe Feld Division
32 Infantry Division

121 Infantry Division

XXVIII Armee Korps

30 Infantry Division
21 Infantry Division
212 Infantry Division
126 Infantry Division
12 Luftwaffe Feld Division

1 (Estonian) Grenzschutz Regiment
2 & 3 (Estonian) Grenzschutz Regiments
4 (Estonian) Grenzschutz Regiment
5 (Estonian) Grenzschutz Regiment
207 Security Division

ARMEE 'NARVA'

Reserves

61 Infantry Division

XXVI Armee Korps

227 Infantry Division
170 Infantry Division

225 Infantry Division

XXXXIII Armee Korps

58 Infantry Division
11 Infantry Division

122 Infantry Division

III Panzer Korps SS

SS Panzergrenadier Division 'Nordland'
20 SS Grenadier Division 'Estonian 1'

2 Luftwaffe Flak Division
285 Security Division

East Pomerania Order of Battle, March 1945

Army Group Vistula

2 Armee (Colonel General Walter Weiß)
XXXXVI Panzer Korps
VII Panzer Korps
XXVII Panzer Korps
XXIII Korps

XVIII Gebirgsjäger Korps
Fortress garrisons of Graudenz & Danzig
Eastern flank of 3.Panzer Armee (reconstituted) (General Erhard Raus)
III (Germanic) SS Panzer Korps
X SS Korps

Red Army

2nd Belorussian Front (Marshal Konstantin Rokossovsky)
Eastern flank of 1st Belorussian Front (Marshal Georgy Zhukov)

3rd Shock Army
1st Guards Tank Army
2nd Guards Tank Army

Order of Battle, 12 April 1945

THIRD PANZER ARMEE

III Panzer Korps SS

11 SS Panzergrenadier Division 'Nordland'
23 SS Panzergrenadier Division 'Nederland'

28 SS Division 'Wallonien'
27 SS Division 'Langemarck'

XXXXVI Panzer Korps

1 Marine Infantry Division
547 Volksgrenadier Division

Gruppe 'Klosseck'

XXXII Armee Korps

281 Infantry Division
Fortress 'Stettin'
549 Volksgrenadier Division

Gruppe 'Voigt'
3 Marine Infantry Division

ARMEE OF EAST PRUSSIA (formerly Second Army)

Reserves
102 Infantry Division
10 Jäger Brigade
349 Volksgrenadier Division
61 Infantry Division
69 Infantry Division
367 Infantry Division

548 Volksgrenadier Division 'Hela'
31 Volksgrenadier Division
4 SS Panzergrenadier Division 'Polizei'
7 Infantry Division
203 Infantry Division
83 Infantry Division

XXIII Armee Korps

4 Panzer Division
252 Infantry Division
12 Luftwaffe Feld Division

35 Infantry Division
23 Infantry Division
32 Infantry Division

XVIII Gebirgs Korps

7 Infantry Division

XXVI Armee Korps

5 Panzer Division (includes remnants
    of 561 Volksgrenadier Division)
21 Infantry Division

1 Infantry Division
58 Infantry Division
28 Jäger Division

IX Armee Korps

93 Infantry Division
95 Infantry Division
561 Volksgrenadier Division

'Grossdeutschland' Panzergrenadier
    Division
14 Infantry Division

Fortress 'Pillau' LV Armee Korps

50 Infantry Division
558 Volksgrenadier Division

286 Infantry Division

VI Armee Korps

129 Infantry Division

170 Infantry Division

Defensive actions Weichselmünde / Werder, April / May 1945

VI Armee Korps
General Horst Großmann. Surrendered to the British 8 May 1945.

170 Infantry Division
General Siegfried Haß. Surrendered to the British on 11 May 1945. Remnants of the division surrendered to the Russians at Hela. Another group managed to escape and surrender to the British at Kiel.

Panzergrenadier Division Großdeutschland
General Karl Lorenz. Surrendered to the British on 10 May 1945. Remnants of the division evacuated in Schleswig Holstein and surrendered to the British.

28 Jäger Division
General Ernst König and later by General Siegfried Verhein. Surrendered to the Soviets on 9 May 1945 in the Weichselmünde.

IX Armee Korps
General Rolf Wuthmann. Surrendered to the Soviets in the Samland on 20 April 1945.

XVIII Gebirgs Korps
General Friedrich Hochbaum. Surrendered to the Soviets in the Weichselmünde.

7 Infantry Division
General Rudolf Noack. Surrendered to the Soviets in May 1945.

XXIII Armee Korps
General Walter Melzer. Surrendered to the Soviets on 8 May 1945 in the Weichselmünde.

12 (Luftwaffe) Feld Division
General Franz Schlieper. Surrendered to the Soviets on 9 May 1945.

23 Infantry Division
General Hans Schirmer. Surrendered to the Soviets in May 1945.

32 Infantry Division
General Hans Boeckh-Behrens. Surrendered to the Soviets on Hela peninsula on 8 May 1945.

35 Infantry Division
General Johann Georg Richert. Surrendered to the Soviets in May 1945.

558 Volksgrenadier Division
General Werner von Bercken. Surrendered to the Soviets on 28. April 1945.

215 Infantry Division
Surrendered to the Russians in the Weichselmünde in May 1945.

252 Infantry Division
General Paul Dreckmann. Surrendered to the Allies on 15 July 1945.

4 Panzer Division
General Clemens Betzel. Killed in Danzig on 27 March 1945. General Ernst Wilhelm Hoffmann was commander until 1 April 1945 and surrendered to the Red Army.

Defensive Actions Hela, April / May 1945

Korps Hela
General Karl Wilhelm Specht. Surrendered to the Russians at Hela in May 1945.

31 Infantry Division
General Anton Manold. Surrendered to the Red Army in May 1945.

203 Infantry Division
General Fritz Gaedicke. Surrendered to the Russians at Hela in May 1945.

Fortress Königsberg, March/April 1945

Fortress Königsberg
Commander General Otto Lasch. Surrendered to the Soviets in Königsberg on 10 April 1945.

61 Volksgrenadier Division
General Rudolf Sperl. Surrendered to the Soviets in Königsberg on 10 April 1945.

69 Infantry Division
General Kaspar Völker. Surrendered to the Soviets in Königsberg on 10 April 1945.

367 Infantry Division
General Hermann Haehnle. Surrendered to the Soviets in Königsberg on 8 April 1945.

548 Volksgrenadier Division
General Erich Sudau. Killed in action at Königsberg on 9 April 1945.

Kampfgruppe Schuberth
SS-Brigadeführer Fritz Schuberth. Killed by a grenade in a bunker at Königsberg on the night of 9/10 April 1945.

Defensive Operations Samland / Pillau / Frische Nehrung, March / April 1945

Armee Samland

XXVIII Armee Korps
General Hans Gollnick. Surrendered to the British in April 1945.

XXVI Armee Korps
General Gerhard Matzky. Surrendered to the British in April 1945.

LV Armee Korps
General Kurt Chill. Surrendered to the Allies on 12 May 1945.

1 Infantry Division
General Henning von Thadden. Wounded on 26 April 1945 in the Samland. Transported to Denmark and died of wounds on 18 May 1945.

5 Panzer Division
General Günther Hoffmann-Schönborn. Injured in battle and evacuated to Denmark. Remnants of the division surrendered to the Soviets in April 1945.

14 Infantry Division
General Gerhard Kircher. Surrendered to the Soviets in Stutthof in May 1945.

22 Infantry Division
General Karl Koetz. Remnants of the division including members of the original divisional staff reached Schleswig-Holstein on 4 May 1945.

50 Infantry Division
General Georg Haus. Killed on 18 April 1945 at Kaddinghagen on the Frische Nehrung. General Kurt Domansky replaced Haus but was killed on 28 April 1945 on the Frische Nehrung. Remnants of the division withdrew and amalgamated with other units on the Frische Nehrung in late April 1945.

58 Infantry Division
General Curt Siewert. Surrendered to the British on 4 May 1945.

83 Infantry Division
General Maximilian Wengler. Killed in action at Pillau on 26 April 1945. Division evacuated to Pillau from Hela on 24–25 April 1945. The division was destroyed in the battle of Pillau on 25–26 April 1945.

93 Infantry Division
General Kurt Domansky. Remnants of the division were integrated in other units including 50 Infantry Division on Frische Nehrung in late April 1945.

95 Infantry Division
General Joachim-Friedrich Lang. Killed on 16 April 1945 in Lochstädter Wald, near Pillau. Remnants of the division were integrated in other units.

551 Volksgrenadier Division
General Siegfried Verhein. Wounded at Pillau on 19 April and remnants of the division withdrew to Frische Nehrung. It was later integrated into 28 Jäger Division.

561 Volksgrenadier Division
General Felix Bexster. The division was destroyed in the Samland. Remnants withdrew to the Frische Nehrung in late April 1945.

Fortress Commandant of Pillau
General Max Horn. Surrendered to the British on 6 May 1945.

Defensive Operations West Prussia / Danzig / Vistula bridgehead, March/April 1945

VII Panzer Korps
General Mortimer von Kessel. Surrendered to the Americans on 2 May 1945.

7 Panzer Division
General Karl Mauß. Badly wounded on 25 March north of Danzig in the area of Oxhöft. Evacuated to Denmark. General Hans Christern replaced Mauß on 25 March 1945. Remnants of the division were evacuated to Swinemünde in April 1945 and then underwent a refit at Krampnitz. The division surrendered in May 1945.

73 Infantry Division
General Franz Schlieper. The divisional staff were evacuated from Hela on 16 April 1945, but most drowned with refugees onboard the freighter 'Goya'. Remnants of the division were integrated in other units.

227 Infantry Division
General Ernst Ratz. The division was destroyed on the Tucheler Heide in West Prussia. Remnants of the division were transferred to Swinemünde in April 1945.

542 Volksgrenadier Division
General Karl Löwrick. Killed in an accident in the Vistula bridgehead on 8 April 1945. Division disbanded during the month of April 1945.

Division Hela East

General Eugen-Alexander Lobach. Injured on 9 April 1945. Remnants of the division finally surrendered on 9 May 1945.

Fortress-Division Danzig (January–March 1945)

General Walter Freytag. Surrendered to the Russians on 8 May 1945.

Gruppe Gümbel Fortress Gotenhafen

General Karl Gümbel. Surrendered to the Allies on 10 May 1945.

Evacuated & destroyed units, January–April 1945

56 Infantry Division

Destroyed in the Heiligenbeil cauldron in March 1945. Remnants escaped to Pomerania.

102 Infantry Division

Destroyed in the Heiligenbeil cauldron in March 1945. Remnants were absorbed by 28 Jäger Division. Some units managed to retreat to Western Pomerania where it formed Division Gruppe 102.

131 Infantry Division

Destroyed in the Heiligenbeil cauldron in March 1945. Remnants escaped to Pomerania.

215 Infantry Division

General Bruno Frankewitz. The division was destroyed in battles on the Tucheler Heide and Gotenhafen in March 1945. Remnants were absorbed into the 32 Infantry Division in early April 1945.

251 Infantry Division

The division was disbanded in March 1945. The staff was transferred to Swinemünde.

286 Infantry Division

Destroyed at Neukuhren in the Samland in April 1945. Remnants integrated into 95 Infantry Division. Staff evacuated to Swinemünde in April 1945.

292 Infantry Division

Destroyed in the Heiligenbeil cauldron in March 1945. Remnants were integrated into 170 Infantry Division in April 1945.

337 Volksgrenadier Division

Destroyed at Danzig. Remnants were integrated into 391 Defence Division. On 11 April 1945 it was destroyed in the Halbe pocket.

349 Volksgrenadier Division
Destroyed in the Heiligenbeil cauldron in March 1945. Remnants were integrated into 21 Infantry Division in April 1945.

389 Infantry Division
Defensive actions in Danzig and West Prussia. Division evacuated to Swinemünde in early April 1945

541 Volksgrenadier Division
Division destroyed in Heiligenbeil cauldron in March 1945. Remnants evacuated to Swinemünde.

547 Volksgrenadier Division
Destroyed in East Prussia in late January 1945. Remnants were integrated into 170 Infantry Division in February 1945.

549 Volksgrenadier Division
Destroyed in East Prussia in late January 1945. Remnants reformed at Pasewalk in Pomerania.

562 Volksgrenadier Division
General Helmuth Hufenbach. Killed on 27 March 1945. The division was destroyed in the Heiligenbeil cauldron.

2 Panzergrenadier Division 'Hermann Göring'
Destroyed in Heiligenbeil cauldron in March 1945. Remnants evacuated in early April 1945.

18 Panzergrenadier Division
Destroyed in the Heiligenbeil cauldron. A new 18 Panzergrenadier Division was built from elements of the original in late March 1945.

24 Panzer Division
General Gustav-Adolf von Nostitz-Wallwitz. Badly wounded on 25 March 1945 in the Heiligenbeil cauldron. Division was destroyed.

4 SS Panzergrenadier Division Polizei
The division was shipped from Hela to Swinemünde in April 1945.

Notes

Notes

Notes

Notes

Notes

Notes

Notes